REPLACEMENT

ACK!

ICKY, STICKY, GROSS STUFF UNDERGROUND

by Pam Rosenberg

illustrated by Beatriz Helena Ramos

ABOUT THE AUTHOR:

Pam Rosenberg lives in Arlington Heights, Illinois, with a husband, two kids, two cats, a hermit crab, a few bugs, and lots of bacteria and other tiny things she doesn't like to think about.

ABOUT THE ILLUSTRATOR:

Beatriz Helena Ramos is an artist from Venezuela who lives and plays in NYC. She works from her animation studio, Dancing Diablo, where she directs animated spots. Beatriz has illustrated a dozen books and she particularly loves gross stories.

The Child's World

Published in the United States of America
by The Child's World®
1980 Lookout Drive • Mankato, MN 56003-1705
800-599-READ • www.childsworld.com

Acknowledgments
The Child's World®: Mary Berendes, Publishing Director
The Design Lab: Kathleen Petelinsek, Design and Page Production
Red Line Editorial: Editing

Photo Credits
iStockphoto.com/Nancy Nehring: cover; Louise Murray/Alamy: 8;
Peter Arnold, Inc./Alamy: 12; Rod Planck/Photo Researchers Inc.: 18

Library of Congress Cataloging-in-Publication Data
Rosenberg, Pam.
  Ack! icky, sticky, gross stuff underground/by Pam Rosenberg;
illustrated by: Beatriz Helena Ramos.
      p. cm. —(Icky, sticky, gross-out books)
  Includes index.
  ISBN-13: 978-1-59296-900-5 (library bound : alk. paper)
  ISBN-10: 1-59296-900-3 (library bound : alk. paper)
  1. Burrowing animals—Juvenile literature. 2. Underground ecology—
Juvenile literature. I. Ramos, Beatriz Helena, ill. II. Title.
  QL756.15.R67 2007
  577.5'84—dc22   2007000408

CONTENTS

4   Ants and Termites

6   The Bat Cave

9   Noisy Insects

10   Smelly Animals

11   Bad Bacteria

13   Creepy Corpses

17   Monstrous Moles

19   Weird Worms

22   Glossary
24   For More Information
24   Index

YOU'RE HAVING A PICNIC WHEN SUDDENLY YOU'RE INVADED BY AN ARMY OF ANTS. They start carrying away bits of your food. You wonder where they're going, so you follow them. They crawl underground. You start to wonder what else is down there along with the ants and part of your lunch. GRAB A SHOVEL AND JOIN ME FOR A JOURNEY UNDERGROUND!

Ants and Termites

Many kinds of ants live in nests underground. These social creatures **live in colonies that can have hundreds of thousands of ants.** But sometimes a colony grows even larger. Scientists found one colony of ants in Japan that was thought to have about **306 million worker ants** and about 1 million queen ants (the ones that can have baby ants). All of these ants were living in more than **40,000 nests** that were connected to one another. Another "super colony" of interconnected nests was discovered in Europe in 2002. **It stretched for more than 3,728 miles** (6,000 kilometers)! Another super colony was discovered in Australia in 2004. It is more than 62 miles (100 km) wide. **Imagine having a picnic near one of those ant colonies!**

There are about **10,000 different kinds of ants** in the world. **There are about one million ants for every person in the world.** It is estimated that if you added up the weight of all of the ants in the world it is equal to the weight of all the humans in the world.

Another insect that lives underground is the **termite.** Termites feed on moist wood and can do a lot of damage to homes. Some kinds of termites build huge mounds out of the earth. **Some mounds in Africa are as much as 30 feet (9 meters) tall!**

The Bat Cave

Caves are underground chambers that have been carved out of rock over millions of years. They are a great place to see rock formations. They are also a great place to see bats! Some caves are home to lots of bats. After flying around at night, they come home to **roost** in their caves. You might see them hanging upside down from the ceiling of the cave. **Bracken Cave is home to about 20 million bats!** It is located near San Antonio, Texas. If you go there as the sun is setting, you can watch **huge swarms of bats** come flying out of the mouth of the cave.

If that isn't creepy enough to keep you out of bat caves, here's some more information. Bats eat—a lot. **Many bats eat half of their own body weight in insects each night.** It is estimated that the bats that live in Bracken Cave **eat 200 tons of insects** each night. **Eating all that food means that bats do something else a lot— poop!** The floor of a bat cave is covered with the stuff. Bat poop even has a special name—**guano.** What keeps the guano from piling up? A bug called the **guano beetle lives on the floor of the caves and eats bat poop.**

Want to know one more **creepy fact** about bat caves? Another kind of beetle, the **dermestid beetle,** eats **the dead bats** that have fallen to the floor of the cave. They can **eat a freshly-fallen bat in just minutes.** Researchers who study bat caves have to wear protective gear so they don't get attacked by these **flesh-eating beetles.** So here's a question for you: Do you have to be batty to become a bat researcher and want to spend your time in caves filled with poop and flesh-eating beetles?

Noisy Insects

Have you ever heard a very **noisy bug** outside? Chances are it was a cicada. **Cicadas live underground** for most of their lives. Certain kinds of **cicadas emerge from the ground every thirteen or seventeen years,** depending on the exact kind of cicada. The female cicadas lay their eggs in little grooves they carve on twigs. When the eggs hatch, the baby cicadas, known as nymphs, drop to the ground. They tunnel underground and spend the next 13 or 17 years there. Then, either 13 or 17 years later, hordes of these insects emerge from underground at the same time. **Imagine as many as a million 1-inch-long (2.5-centimeter-long) cicadas covering an acre of land, all with big, bulging, red eyes!**

Smelly
Animals

Many skunks spend some of their time underground. They dig burrows in the ground for dens. If you've seen skunks in the area, you might want to be very careful before checking out a hole in the ground. It may be an entrance to a skunk's home. And, you probably already know what skunks do when they are threatened— **they spray a nasty-smelling liquid at you. This liquid is stored in two glands—one on either side of their anus.** What's an anus, you ask? It's a fancy name for the hole that an animal's poop comes out of. When skunks decide to spray, they can hit targets more than 10 feet (3 meters) away. The smell of this stinky liquid can be detected up to a mile away!

Bad Bacteria

Did you know that the dirt under your feet contains **millions of bacteria**? You can't see them without a **microscope**, but they are there. Most of them are **helpful** and perform jobs like **breaking down dead plants and animals.** Without them, we'd all be wading through dead stuff every time we stepped outside!

But some bacteria can make us sick. **One kind of bacteria that is commonly found in dirt is Clostridium tetani.** This nasty little guy can get into your body through a cut or other wound. Once inside it starts to multiply. The original bacteria and all its little friends start produce a **neurotoxin**—a poison that affects your nervous system. What happens next? **You get a disease called tetanus.** Your muscles start having really strong spasms. These spasms can be so forceful that they can tear your muscles and even cause your bones to break! If you don't get treatment, you can even die. Prevention is simple—make sure you get all the **tetanus shots** your doctor recommends.

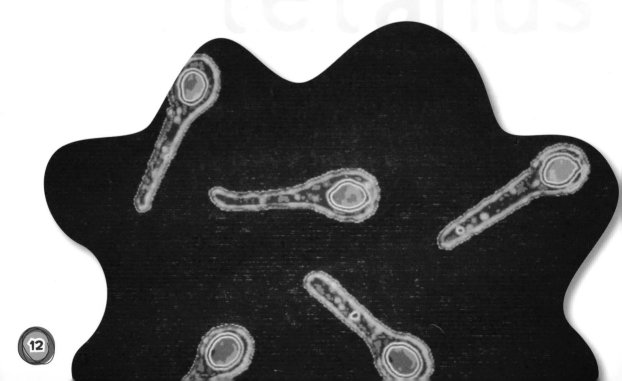

Creepy Corpses

corpse corpse corpse

Remember what we said about bacteria breaking down dead plants and animals? Human **corpses** count as dead animals. **Our bodies are filled with bacteria** when we are alive. Lots of them live inside our **intestines** and help break down our food. **They don't die** when **we die; they stay alive and start to break down the dead cells** of our intestines. These living **bacteria start breaking down our bodies even before they are buried underground.** Then they keep feeding on the dead cells after we're buried. Soon some of them start invading other parts of the body. Chemicals released by the dead cells also help speed the process. **After about a year, all that is left** is the **skeleton and teeth with tiny bits of tissue left on them.**

The ancient Egyptians had a special way of preparing the bodies of their dead for burial. They **removed as much moisture as possible from the corpse.** A dried out corpse doesn't decay easily. First, the internal parts that would decay easily were removed. Many of the body organs were removed through a cut made in the left side of the abdomen. But removal of the brain was more difficult. Special hooked tools were pushed up through the nostrils of the corpse. Then **bits of the brain were grabbed with the hooked end of the tool** and pulled back out through the nose. **The only organ that wasn't removed from the dead body was the heart. A special kind of salt was then used to dry out the body.** Once the drying process was complete, **the corpse was wrapped in linen strips.**

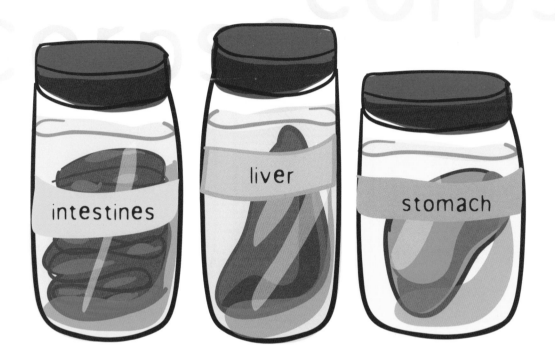

intestines

liver

stomach

Have you ever gone to a museum to see an exhibit on ancient Egypt? If you have, you may have seen **special jars called canopic jars.** The **stomach, liver, lungs,** and **intestines** of the **dead person** were preserved in those jars and buried with the **mummified body.**

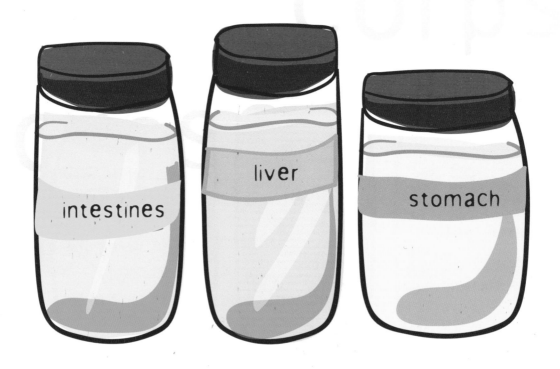

intestines

liver

stomach

The **internal organs of dead people** from later time periods in Egyptian history were **taken out, dried out, and wrapped up.** They were then **put back inside the body** before it was wrapped. The canopic jars were still buried with the body, but there were no body parts inside them.

Monstrous Moles

No, not the little dark bumps that grow on your skin. Moles are small animals that spend most of their time underground. **They can't see very well,** but they have a **great sense of touch and hearing.** The tip of a mole's muzzle has lots of microscopic structures that **help it to feel its way around underground. Earthworms are a favorite food of many moles.**

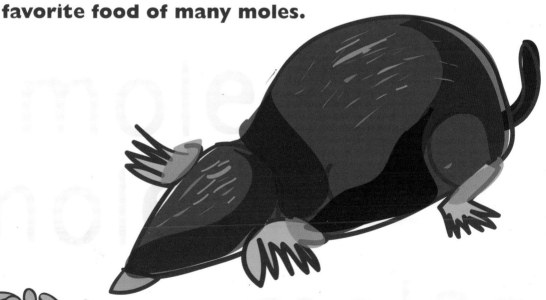

All moles are a bit strange looking, but one kind that is really odd-looking is the **star-nosed mole.** This creature lives in the eastern part of North America. It looks like other moles except that it has a hairless nose surrounded by a ring of twenty-two fleshy, pink **tentacles**. Picture something that looks a little bit like a rat with big feet and pink fingers sticking out all around its nose. **When it is looking for food, it uses those fleshy tentacles to feel** its surroundings. They move so quickly that they can touch twelve objects per second. **They can identify and eat prey so quickly that you can't see them do it!**

Weird Worms

We already know that moles like to eat earthworms. Lots of other animals do, too. But did you know that **some people eat earthworms?** They are a great source of **protein**. Now who'd like some tasty fried earthworms? **Yum!**

Did you know that earthworms have male and female reproductive parts? Two earthworms get together and each one fertilizes the eggs of the other one. The fertilized eggs are deposited in the ground in tiny cocoons that are about the size of a grain of rice. **Tiny baby worms come out of their cocoons in two to four weeks.**

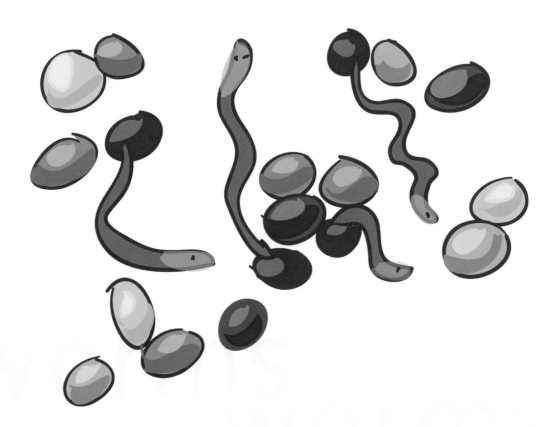

You might think that **worms are creepy or gross.**
After all, they are brown and kind of slimy and they crawl
around in dirt all day. But these **creepy crawlers
tunnel through the soil bringing air to the
deep layers. Worms eat lots of waste—and
they poop a lot themselves! Worm
poop helps make the
soil better** for growing things. So remember:
The earthworm (and some of its underground neighbors)
may not be pretty, but they have important work to do!

GLOSSARY

bacteria (bak-TEER-ee-uh) Bacteria are microscopic living things. Billions of bacteria live in dirt.

cicada (sih-KAY-duh) A cicada is a large insect with a wide head and transparent wings. Cicadas spend much of their lives underground.

colony (KOL-uh-nee) A colony is a large group of insects that live together. A very large colony of ants was discovered in Europe.

corpses (KORPS-ez) Corpses are dead bodies. Bacteria eat the flesh of corpses.

gear (GEER) Gear is equipment or clothing that is used for a special purpose. Scientists who study bat caves wear protective gear to protect themselves from flesh-eating beetles.

intestines (in-TESS-tinz) Intestines are the internal organs that digest food after it leaves the stomach. Many bacteria live inside human intestines.

microscope (MY-kruh-skope) A microscope is a tool with powerful lenses that magnify very small things so they can be seen and studied. You need a microscope to see bacteria and other tiny living things.

muzzle (MUZ-uhl) The nose, mouth, and jaws of an animal are its muzzle. Moles have microscopic organs on their muzzles that help them feel their way around underground.

neurotoxin (NOOR-oh-toks-in) A neurotoxin is a poison that acts on the nervous system. The bacteria that cause tetanus produce a neurotoxin in the human body.

nostrils (NOSS-truhlz) Nostrils are the two openings in the nose used for breathing and smelling. The ancient Egyptians removed the brains from dead bodies through the nostrils.

protein (PRO-teen) Protein is a substance that is found in all living animal and plant cells. Earthworms are high in protein.

roost (ROOST) When an animal roosts, it settles somewhere to sleep or rest. Bats roost in their caves during the day.

tentacles (TEN-tuh-kuhlz) Tentacles are long, fleshy limbs used by some animals for feeling, moving, or grabbing things. A star-nosed mole has a ring of pink tentacles around its nose.

FOR MORE INFORMATION

Delafosse, Claude, and Daniel Moignot. *Let's Look at Animals Underground.* London: Moonlight, 1998.

Lauber, Patricia, and Todd Telander (illustrator). *Earthworms, Underground Farmers.* New York: Henry Holt, 1997.

Perry, Phyllis. *Animals Under the Ground.* New York: Franklin Watts, 2001.

INDEX

Africa, 5
ants, 4, 5
Australia, 4
bacteria, 11, 12, 13
bats, 6, 7, 8
Bracken cave, 6, 7
burrows, 10
canopic jars, 15, 16
caves, 6, 7, 8
cicadas, 9
cocoons, 20
corpses, 13, 14, 15, 16
dermestid beetle, 8
earthworms, 17, 19, 20
eggs, 9, 20
Egyptians, 14
flesh-eating beetles, 8
guano beetle, 7

guano, 7
insects, 7, 8, 9
intestines, 13, 15
Japan, 4
moles, 17, 18
mummies, 14, 15, 16
nervous system, 12
North America, 18
poop, 7, 8, 10, 21
skeleton, 13
skunks, 10
smells, 10
star-nosed mole, 18
tentacles, 18
termites, 4, 5
tetanus, 12
Texas, 6
worms, 17, 19, 20, 21